The Pain Book. copyright © 2017 by A. B. Rose.

All rights reserved. Printed in the United States of America. This book or any portion thereof may not be reproduced or used in any manner whatsoever without the written permission of the publisher except in the case of reprints in the context of reviews.

Cover Art provided by Frank Scialabba (@francis_joseph1).

ISBN-13: 978-0-692-97428-5

This book contains the words && thoughts I never believed I would be able to share. Hopefully this inspires you to do the same.

Dedicated to all those who played a role in orchestrating this Romantic Tragedy. Thank you for the inspiration.

[The Prelude].

So much pain,
so much despair,
neatly compiled & organized,
onto these simple pages.

As if I could, somehow, make sense of all this.

This ink bleeds
down the skin of these pages,
as I sit here revising,
tirelessly,
torn between using **the words I need to say**,
and the ones that I'm brave enough to use.

I don't know if I'm good enough
to give this story the justice it deserves.

If my pain is left misunderstood,
if I can't ever be honest with myself,
and with all of you,
then it, truly, was all for nothing.

I, still, don't know if it's good enough,
but this will have to do.

"If you bring forth what is within you, what you bring forth will save you. If you do not bring forth what is within you, what you do not bring forth will destroy you."
      Gospel of Thomas, Verse 70.

[No].

No, I don't write about things that rhyme,
I write about pain and lost time.

My writing is not that kind,
instead, it's rather snide.
Get it?
Not-that-kind,
Yet, still,
Not that kind.

I write about heartache and sorrow,
Fearing a bunch of empty tomorrows.

I don't write in the most eloquent nature,
in fact, my writing is, sometimes, filled with hatred.

I just scribble these words on a pad,
hoping that someone out there will feel bad,
or feel mad,
or feel anything at all.

After all, isn't that what this life is all about,
Feeling?
I'm not talking about feeling something in the physical,
but in the metaphorical,
in the psychological;
Feeling those things they call "emotions".

Isn't that why we all write?
Isn't that why you all read?
Aren't you just like me,
Just looking for the right words that will make it all okay.

[Desecration].

We traded trust for lust
&& now none of it means anything
at all.

[Broken Together].

You think you're broken.
Well, me too.
Let's be broken together.

Let's put these broken pieces together.

[Growing Pains].

What is the truest measurement of age?

Is it Time or is it Pain?

Cuz I've got all this pain
stored deep inside my brain
that I could never explain
to anyone by another name,
and now I think
I'm too fucked up to change.

And this thing they call age,
Is nothing more than a cage,
Something to define you,
Something to confine you,
Something to label you,
But they don't really know you,
They don't know what you've been through.

Don't ask me about my age,
Ask me about my pain.

[Wisdom].

My grandmother used to always say:
Save your money,
Don't spend on things you don't need.

Funny, as I look back,
I must have misconstrued her message.
Because now I see,
It was not only about wasted money,
It was not only about worthless things.

Now, I have learned.
I've spent myself into bankruptcy.

I've spent all my time,
I've spent all my energy,
I've spent all my emotions,
on someone I didn't need.

[Courage].

To write down these thoughts,
To express these emotions,
To reveal oneself,
in the most authentic,
and unrehearsed way,
is a courageous thing.

Most people are too afraid to even feel them.

[Plans Go Awry].

We're rarely who we think we are && almost never, exactly, who we planned to be.

[Villain].

Being the Villain is always easier;
no expectations,
no fault or criticisms,
no disappointment,
&& no attachments.

I've decided to become the Villain
that you've always wanted me to be.

[Just a Little...]

You need to be a little mad to show people the things they've never known before.

[The Anarchist].

Embrace the rush of Life's Uncertainty,
&& enjoy the potential for Chaos.

[Innocence Lost].

After all I've done,
After all I've seen,
I can no longer believe,
In anything,
In anyone.

[Slipping away...]

I'm lost & out of touch,
Consumed by agony, about to bust,
The more I grasp, the more I clutch,
It feels as though everything I love,
Disintegrates into dust.

[Voluntary Slavery].

We wear the chains of our past,
Until we **find** the power,
To liberate **ourselves**.

I didn't know I was wearing so many chains.
I didn't know that my chains
wore such innocent disguises.

But I have been a slave for so long.

I have served a long sentence,
Riddled with persecution & regret.
I almost forgot what a life of freedom felt like.

Ironic
because I have no one to blame,
except for myself.

Maybe part of me enjoyed
bearing the weight of your burden.

Maybe part of me enjoyed
this **Voluntary Slavery**.

[Unstable].

My chemical compounds are unstable.
My psychological makeup is unstable.

I am combustible,
I am poisonous,
I am explosive.

They say that change is a sign of progression,
But, **I will kill** for some stability.

[The Price of Poetry].

A poet can never be a true poet, as we know him to be, without some misery to hold onto.

[Broken Pieces].

They shattered the glass
that so delicately cradled
all of my life's hopes & dreams.

And as I fell to my knees,
trying to pick up those **broken pieces,**

I saw my own reflection
in that broken mess,
and found who I truly was.

[Masks].

You don't really know me,
for you know nothing of my past.
So, when you look at me, now,
all you can see is my mask.

[Fearful Inhibitions].

Life is hard,
and full of mistakes.

Plagued with regrets,
and chances we never take.

[Inspiration].

From the Concrete, arose,
a lovely, wretched flower, a Rose.
Adorned with thorns,
Painted with pain,
a fierce, intoxicatingly sinful, deep red.

As red as the blood that has been spilt,
as red as her lips, so lush,
the color of love,
the color of sin.

This lonely Rose came from nothing,
nothing but a crack in the earth,
a dark, forgotten crack,
where sunlight could not reach,
where water would not flow,
where the soil was absent of any nutrient.

Still, this Rose arose,
from some deathly hallows, so it goes.
Still, it grew high and lush,
attracting the sight of every passerby.

But what did the audience see
as their eyes were met with such a sight?
They saw nothing but plight, stricken with fright.
This Rose had scared all the onlookers away,
this Rose just had too many thorns,
nobody would stay.

No one would stay to look on at this Rose,
to admire all that it has gained,
and how far it has come

from such humble beginnings.
The triumph that this Rose had enjoyed
meant nothing to the ignorant audience,
for they had not seen what it took to grow,
they knew not what it took to overcome such circumstances.

All they could see was a thorny Rose,
risen up from a dirty sidewalk,
threatening too much danger,
and offering not enough beauty.

Stuck in that crack,
they knew it would never escape.

And then, one day,
that Rose passed away.

Nobody gave a fuck anyway.

[Nameless].

Hello,
How are you?
Who am I?
Oh, I must apologize,
I haven't properly introduced myself.

You don't know me,
you probably never will.
I am just another amongst this faceless crowd,
but that's the way I like it,
that is where I feel most safe.

I like to hide amongst the rest of them,
although, I am nothing like the rest of them,
morphing and contorting myself
into the shape of them,
into the form of whatever is deemed most "acceptable".

My defense mechanisms are like that of a Chameleon,
I blend in with my environment
to conceal myself from the predators,
from anyone who may spot something unusual in me.
For, I am, indeed, unusual.

From grade school
they teach us to pick out the one that is not like the rest,
to detect uniqueness,
to detect difference,
and to chastise it.

We see it on our tests.
We see it on the playground.
We see it, ubiquitously, throughout our lives,
because this is how we've been engineered.

We are not safe.
Those, like me, are not safe.
That is why we must hide,
conform,
become sycophantic & artificial,
like the rest of them.
That is the only way to preserve ourselves,
but, in the same token,
the same way to lose ourselves.

Because, inevitably, we may lose ourselves in this portrayal.
We may forget what it is like to be,
so unique,
after a lifetime of repressing these qualities,
in an attempt to gain acceptance,
in an attempt to hide from these predators.

I'm sorry,
I must go now.
I fear they may be onto me,
I think I hear them coming,
I feel their stares on the back of my neck.
I must be going, now,
but thank you for lending your ear.

My name?
Don't worry about my name,
for I am Nobody,
yet, I am Everybody,
Just like you.
We are the same.

I'm just here to deliver the messages
that you've been dying to hear.

[22].

At the age of 22 years,
I realize I must have been looking at Love all wrong.

Maybe we shouldn't be looking at Love,
With any type of ownership or attachment.

I think we need to abandon all feelings of attachment,
This way, you can never, really, lose,
Something that was never yours.

We must enjoy it while it's there,
Embrace it while it lasts,
&& let it go when it's gone.

Love will do nothing but cloud your vision,
Corrupt your judgment,
&& bring you to your knees.

The only Love that we truly need is for ourselves.

[Darker].

I'm a bit Darker than the average,
but, then again,
we should never aim to just be average.

["Fit In"].

I never fit in,
I just pretended to.

    — A. B. Rose.

[Martyr].

I deserved this.
I wanted this.

I know you can't understand it,
but, I did this for you.

Lash out,
keep going
until it doesn't hurt anymore.
Punish me until we're both numb.

Nail up my hands,
and don't forget my feet.
Adorn my head with a crown of thorns,
for I am The Rose, grown from the concrete.

Hate me.
Hate me.
Hate me.
I am your Martyr.

[Self-Destructive].

Self-destructive habits are always the hardest to identify in ourselves.

[Re-finding What was Lost].

I'm still the same underneath
all this bullshit.

If I can just get through this,
maybe I could find myself again.

If I can just get through this,
maybe I could figure out,
exactly where it was
that I got so Lost.

One Man [Can Change].

They say,
One Man can change the world,
but, not until
the world changes that One Man.

Once upon a time,
a wise man,
more accurately,
a drunken, very, lost man,
told me,
"A child is born with a heart of gold.
The weight of the world turns it cold".

I believe he was right.
Perplexed,
I wondered how such insight,
such vision,
could be aroused from such a decrepit vessel.

But, isn't that how it goes?
You can only learn from the pain.

You only learn from being
worn down,
broken down,
bearing the weight of the world,
until you, too, become
Decrepit,
Broken,
Drunk,
Alone.

This is my journey,
These are my 'steps'.

Unfortunately for Us,
the ones like me,
we don't know how many
of these steps
we need to take.

We don't know what is necessary of Us
to find the Truth.

But, what I do know
is that there is a lesson behind each failure,
in each heartache,
&& in every moment of pain.

It is left to me
to translate
and transcribe
these lessons of agony,
presented in an inconceivable language,
in order to write my own happy ending.

It is only through
this pain,
this struggle,
this change,
that this One Man
will change the world.

They [Left].

They have left
so many words
Unsaid.

They have left
so many truths
Unsaid.

Is it because of guilt,
or for the preservation of a false identity?

People are fucked up && selfish in their motives.

They've scared me into never loving again.

Don't bother with Love,
it will only bring Pain.

[Self-Deprecation].

I'm writing this with a cigarette in hand,
in an effort to hurt myself
just a little bit more.

I probably deserve it.

[Scars].

What would we be without these scars?
Nothing but a piece of flesh.

It is the scars,
that make us who we are.

[Brainwashed].

I was told I'm bad,
I was told I'm mean,
I was told I'm heartless,
I was taught to be a Villain.

Should I believe the lies,
that bolster this malicious vendetta?
Or should I listen to the voice
six inches between my ears?

The voice tells me that we know better.
He says, "we always knew that they could never understand"
He was right,
I always knew.
But, the part of me that is still human
couldn't resist the temptations of hope and bliss.

Is it so wrong for me to crave the happiness
that they all seem to reap so effortlessly?
the happiness that comes with a life of ignorance,
the joy that lies in the simplicity of a mortal existence.

Is there no happiness for a Villain like me?
Maybe for a moment or two,
but, then it's gone,
just like the rest of them.

I knew long ago
that this journey must be walked alone.

No yellow brick road,
just a long, eroded, desolate wasteland,
leading me to somewhere only He knows.

But He told me that this is where I was meant to go.
He told me that this is how it was meant to be.

For, this journey, this life, is not my own.
I was created for a purpose outside of myself.

I realize, now, that I am the foolish one.
I was never meant for prolonged happiness,
a moment here and there is all that I'm given,
just enough to keep me going,
just enough to keep me from letting it all go.

There is no happiness for a Villain.
They simply won't allow it.
So, my journey continues,
a pilgrimage comparable to a perverted masquerade.

I am forced to wear these masks,
the ones that I was told to put on,
for, I cannot fulfill this destiny in my true form.
They have always been afraid of what they don't understand.

When Galileo told them that the world was round,
they sentenced him to death.
When Mr. King spoke for the equality of man,
they put a bullet in his brain.
When Christ spoke of salvation and forgiveness,
He was crucified and tortured in the company of other Villains.

So, that leads us here.
We have learned from our previous mistakes,
change cannot be achieved in our true form.

We have to blend in with them,
Sin as they sin,
Lie as they lie,
Destroy as they destroy.
It's the only way.

I know all of this,
I've always known,
but it still hurts.

I did not sign up for this.
I did not raise my hand.
I am no volunteer.

I was chosen for glory,
and so much more pain.

Many days I ask for you to reconsider your choice,
maybe there is someone more fit for this,
someone who is not as weak as I.

I've come so far, through so much,
but you've shown me how much more is left to go.

And although I know I can make it to the end,
being carried upon your shoulders,

each time I must fall,
I get up slower,
never the same.

Forever changed by the pain.

He said that pain is necessary
to understand the broken.
He said that pain was priceless,
the only way to buy yourself into
the Kingdom of Glory.
He said that the pain, here, would be nothing
compared to salvation that awaits.

But I don't want to make it through any more.
I don't want to bear this cross any longer,
dragging it through the city,
as they laugh,
as they snicker,
as they stone me.

I plead with them,
try to show them who I really am,
and who I'm really not,
but they'll never see it.

He said it would all play out like this.

And in the midst of their rejection,
my faith is restored.

I know the pain is part of my metamorphosis,
but, truthfully, I'm afraid of what I am to become
as a result of this journey.

Again, I must plead,
please, pick someone else to be your Villain.

[Free-Will].

'Free-will' they say,
But what's so "free" about it?
It comes at a price,
And there's nothing free about it.

You think you chose this,
But you didn't.
It was already chosen,
Or, at least, influenced.
Maybe they didn't have their finger on the trigger,
But, they, most certainly,
Loaded the clip for you.

You think I just chose to dedicate my life to 'saving' the world?
Of course not.
I was cursed to spend a lifetime,
Trying to save,
Only the ones who can't be.
So, instead, I embrace this phony altruistic venture,
Towards self affirmation.
Taking on each new case,
Trying to make some kind of difference.

Maybe tonight he won't come home drunk and beat on his kid.

Maybe tonight he won't abused the same woman that loves him.

Maybe this one won't drink himself to death in a cold, dark alleyway.

Who knows?
I don't.
But, at least I'll try.
Not because it is my choice,
but because you made it my choice.

Free-Will, they say,
then why do I feel like a slave to it?

[Impermanence].

Everything in this life is temporary.
No matter how fast you chase,
No matter how hard you clutch on,
it will all escape you in time.

Time is the absolution of existence.
It takes everything with it,
the bad & the good.

Friends,
Family,
Feelings,
Thoughts,
Identities,

Existence, as we know it,
is temporary.

But, don't let that stop you from trying.

[Strength].

What is strength,
and how do we measure it?

In order to qualitatively measure
an essential factor
that largely predicts our successes
and our failures,
we must look beyond our superficial notions,
we must narrow our scope of perception.

Strength is not measured in the physical,
although, it can, undoubtedly, be materialized.

A perplexing thought, isn't it?
Strength is amorphous,
yet, can be manifested into action;
both, nurtured and dwarfed by our thought,
and told through our experience.

What is strength?
Strength is courage.
Strength is will.
Strength is life after pain.
Strength is what is left after security is gone.
Strength is what is left after faith has been reduced to rubble.
Strength is the only option, when there is no option.

Strength requires understanding.
Strength requires courage.
Strength requires acceptance
of what we cannot change,
and the the will to change,
what we can.

Strength is not categorical.
Strength is measured on a continuum.

At times we may be weak,
but each new day
brings new strength,
and a new opportunity to learn from our weaknesses.

Our innate weakness is what makes us beautiful.
Our innate weakness is what makes this life worth living.
What would life be without weakness?
What would life be without adversity?

The beauty of strength is that it will never leave you,
just as so many others will.

It has always been deep inside,
you just have to find it.

[The Rush of Uncertainty].

I'm sitting, calmly,
on a plane
going far, far, away.

The take off is my favorite part,
it must be the rush of mortal uncertainty.

Either this plane rises,
high above the clouds
and into the sunset,
or it crashes,
&& burns to the ground,
leaving nothing but ash.

I would be fine with either outcome.

There will be no trace of our existence.

Sick, isn't it?
To have such an absent appreciation for the gift of life.
They call it a gift,
but, sometimes,
it seems like more of a damnation,
a penalty,
a sentence.

After all,
didn't those hypocritical patriarchs sell us on that idea of purgatory?
Maybe this is it.

The idea is predicated upon the 'guarantee' that something better
exists after this shit hole.
So, against my better judgement,
I'll find security in buying into their narrative.

Isn't that what they intended?

Probably, but not like this.
This is just twisted.
I guess this is what happens
when you've lost all hope.

[Running].

I'm running through these streets,
under the cover of midnight,
in the security of the shadows,
at a time when I know nobody will be around to see.

As thoughts of you run through my mind,
I'm running to try to get you off my mind.

Running is my therapy.
Actually, it's my only option.

I'm too weak to sit in a room and be vulnerable,
even if it is with a stranger.

It makes no difference, really,
everyone is a stranger,
when you live like me.

I'm too cowardly to be myself in a room full of 'friends',
just as I'm too cowardly to sit in an office
and bring my skeletons out of the closet,
to allow the proverbial wolves out of my cellar.
They've been locked away for so long,
They must be so hungry after all this time,
Ravenous for daylight,
Dying for truth.

I've realized that my cowardice is not a result of fearing outside judgment,
or fearing the disapproval of my peers.

I've discovered that my fears lie in the realization of an absolute truth.
I fear that if these words are to be spoken,
there will be no backspace,
No delete,
No undo.

I fear that if the truth is to be spoken,
then it will become absolute.
Once spoken, I cannot go back to pretending.
Once spoken, I have to own it.
Once spoken, I have to accept it,
and I'm just not ready.

Until then,
Let me run through this darkness.

[Peaks && Valleys].

I've reached a few heights,
but, trust me,
I know the lows.

I've spent a lot of time there,
in the lows, that is.
I've practically lived there.

You could say,
I have a timeshare,
in the pits of devastation and loneliness.

Because before each peak,
there is a valley.

And after each peak,
there is a long, lonely fall to the bottom.

I've seen these truths,
and enjoyed the fall from bliss.

What I can tell you after these rights of passage,
is that I am still here,
and I am better because of it.

I am fractured,
I am cracked,
I am damaged,
but I have never been broken.

There have been times,
in the depths of my own despair,
when I truly believed I was broken.

There have been times that I thought
I was ready to give up.

There have been times that I thought
I had nothing left to give.

But then,
just when I thought it was over,
the sun rose again,
and I Rose again.

[High Tide].

I'm drowning in an abyss of **Black**ness.

I'm choked up by this **Black** sea,
simultaneously praying,
that they won't see,
The Black in me.

Hope is a scarcity,
when you live like me.
Fighting to stay afloat,
constantly.

But, before I go under,
for the last time,
You're the last thing,
to cross **my mind**.

[Lost && Found].

These words are mine.
These feelings are mine.
This pain is mine.

So let me have it.

I don't have much these days,
but, at least I have this.

You could never take these words from me,
You could never strip me of this clarity,
You could never undo what has already been done.

This clarity came at a price,
&& it nearly cost me everything I had.

High Tide almost washed me away.

It felt as though the tides were pulling at me,
beckoning me with a relentless call,
attempting to submerge me beneath,
an abyss of emptiness.

I almost lost myself back then,
but I found myself here.

Don't just gloss over these lines,
they mean too much to me.

I said:
I found myself,
Here.

[Low Tide].

I spent so much of my life
searching for someone to save me.

Then, one day,
I decided to stop
looking in all the wrong places,
&& decided to look inside myself.

Finally,
I decided to save myself.

Now I can stand,
on my own.

As I stand in the shallows,
reminiscing on the days
I thought I was drifting away,

It feels like Low Tide.

[Proverbs I].

Always trust your instincts.

Those will prevail && remain unbiased, when the weaker parts of your mind become compromised to Emotion.

[The Battle].

It's always been a battle,
of who could care less.

Ironically,
The Victor and the Loser
are one in the same.

To the Victor goes the spoils,
spoiled with loneliness and contempt.

To the Loser
goes the same Fate.
Nobody is spared.

But to Whom do we owe
the gratitude of such an honor?

Ourselves.
We are the masters
of our own Misery.

Could we stop, if we tried?
Only if we could see through these lies.

But, why stop now?
We've come so far,
there isn't much left.

We can do it if we try,
We can ruin this if we try.

It shouldn't be too hard,
unless we want it to be.
After all, what Choice do we have?

We are merely creatures of habit,
these habits include self-destruction & selfishness.
We can do this if we try.

Don't try.
We can't fix this.
You can't fix me.

[Victim].

I remember the day you told me to,
"**Stop** playing the victim".

This must be a rough day for you,
because, now, I've assembled all these pages,
Just to play the victim,
&& guess who **the** Villain is this time?

Please, forgive my **insanity**.
Isn't it just like me,
to assume a role,
&& become the perfect actor?

[Do you still remember?].

Do you still remember
what it used to feel like so long ago,
when we were both madly in love,
before we knew how much it hurt,
before we knew what it would do to us?

Do you still remember
the feeling of opening one of those letters?
When your heart would drop to the floor
in adoration and excitement for what we might say to eachother?

I still remember.
I think that's why it all still hurts.
I still remember what it felt like.
I still remember what you felt like.
I still remember what it was like to be each others.

Don't you miss that feeling?
I do.

But now I have to make myself forget.
It'll make the pain go easier.

We'll try to forget,
and, eventually, we might even believe we forgot.

We'll move on and pretend like it never happened.
We'll keep going and find something new.

But it won't be the same.
I'll still remember,
and I'll know it's not the same.

[Thief].

I retrace our steps
over in my mind,
endlessly,
trying to find exactly where it was
when all of this fell apart.

I'm trying to pinpoint exactly who,
or what it was,
that changed you into a stranger,

That stole you from me,
stealing my heart & my mind
with you.

[Never Came Back].

I'm restless, I'm uneasy,
I'm broken and I'm needy.
I'm desperate for some closure.
I need something I can hold onto,
because holding you just doesn't feel the same anymore.

I've been beaten down and battered,
my heart, scarred and tattered.
What is left, I cannot be sure.
I can't be sure of what I still have left,
because all I can think about is all that has been lost.

We lie in this bed, beside one another.
We have lied in this bed, to one another.
Proximity means nothing anymore,
when it feels like we're miles apart.
Stop the lies, we just aren't what we once were.

I've spent so much time trying to pretend,
trying to fake a smile and push on,
hoping that tomorrow will bring a better day,
hoping that tomorrow will bring a better you.
But it never does.
You never came back.

You never came back,
from that vacation you took.
It still feels like yesterday,
we were so young, so in love, so happy.

**But you changed,
and now we're none of that.**

We're just empty now.
I'm just empty now.
This is all just empty now.
And now I am left
with only two choices.

To hold onto the wonderful memories of what once was,
and remain empty,
or to let it all go,
and try to become whole again.

[Love&War].

In times of **Love&War,**
You must be willing to ruin it all;
Burn the fields && torch the very village that raised you.

[Now&Then].

You have become a stranger now,
a poor rendition of who you once were.

I am nothing but a shell now,
an empty impersonation of what I once was.

We are nothing now.

And I can't help but wonder,
[How long you've been faking it],
[if any of it was real at all],
if we were [anything][real] at all.

[50].

I used to think that you were something,
Like nothing I've known before.

but now I learned,
the hard way,

that you're just another chapter of the suffering.

You were a lot of Pain,
disguised inside some happiness.

[The 5th].

You know that song
that you used to share with that person
you thought you would spend your life with?

You used to love that song,
it used to fill you with such happiness,
a feeling that money just couldn't buy.

But, now you hate that song.
You change the radio every time it comes on,
you have to remove it from all your playlists
just to keep yourself from falling apart.

I have a bunch of those songs, now,
but the torturous reminders of you don't stop there.
I also have the 5th of September.

Today would have been 8 years
if we could have made it,
but I guess we didn't share in the same vision.

Today is much harder than I thought it would be,
but that's okay, **I'm going to** let it rip me apart,
I'm going to **let myself** wallow in the misery,
Mourning all that we've lost.

Maybe tomorrow I can **let go** of all this hope,
Maybe tomorrow I can let go **of** all the wishing
that you'd go back to **who you used to be**.

[Then, Gone].

The idea of loss is just an illusion,
for you can not lose, that,
which you never really had.

People && things are momentary,
Fleeting,
and then,
G o n e.

[Cold].

The winters are cold here,
but nothing compared to a frozen heart.

Ever since you left,
I've become frost-bitten & numb.

The nights have become filled with deafening silence,
&& my days are much of the same.

When I'm feeling courageous,
I whisper your name,

Just to remember
all that I've lost.

[Proverbs II].

Sometimes, saying nothing is better than saying something.

And yet, sometimes,
they are the exact same.

[Proverbs III].

At the end of it all,
This is all we get to keep,
Just a memory.

[Denial].

Part of me is still trying to get over you,
Though, I know I never will.

[Loose Ends].

I was thinking about you tonight.
I hope that you're doing alright.
I'll make this short, and say that I'm doing just fine.
But not a day goes by that you aren't on my mind.

I hope you think of me when you're all alone.
I pray to see your name each time I look at my phone.
But every ring is followed by the harsh reality
that you're going on without me.

My selfless wish is that you're out there, somewhere, happy,
and that you've forgotten all about me.
That you've moved on, moved forward, but stayed you,
and that you're still **the person I once knew**.

And I hope you don't live with any regret,
wondering what our life could have been,
because I've been dealing with that,
sorting it out with a pad and a pen.

And my conclusion is that there is no end,
no end, to the loose ends of regret.

[Always, Always].

I love that she Always says,
Always.

Reminding me of someone
who is so hopelessly clinging on
to the notions of
Forever.

Yet, she is someone
who willfully & deliberately
abandoned & threw away
Forever.

Life is paradoxical in that way.

People are paradoxical in that way.

Their conscious acts in what seems to be
a calculated && thought-out measure,
although, they remain disillusioned to the truth.

Still, their subconscious has moments of clarity,
shining through, to reveal their true desires,
even if they remain
unbeknownst to the conscious mind.

[Onions].

She hates her onions,
She says they make her cry.

She says they're sour,
And only bring tears.

Funny, it seems,
Because I love onions.

Yes, onions are sour,
Yes, onions do make me cry,

But, sometimes,
I want to cry.

She won't have onions,
Especially in the evenings,

Funny, it seems,
You're my onions in the evenings.

[Reflection].

Maybe it's all tainted.
Maybe it's more of a choice than a destiny.
Maybe it didn't have to be this way,

But, I didn't know any better.
I, still, don't know any better.

[Time].

It's not the nights,
spent alone
in an empty bed,
that kill me.

But, the nights
that I lie awake,
next to you,
are the hardest ones.

Watching the clock,
not knowing how much time,
we, really, have left.

After all,
Time is all that really matters, anyway.

[No More].

The more you love someone,
the more potential you have
to hate that same someone.

Such a shame,
we flipped the script,
and went to shit.
First, it was bliss,
but, now, it's this.

I've sat and cried
from all the lies,
sat and tried
to take it in stride.

But now I'm tired.

The one I admired,
is nothing but a whore.

Just another story,
of a love no more.

[Pain].

No, I don't want to see your pity,
I want the guilt to eat you alive,
late at night, when you're all alone,
as you reflect on all that you've thrown away.

I want you to mourn the death of two failed dreams.
I want you to feel this, as I have.
I want you to lose sleep, as I have.
I want you to die in the loneliest moments of 3am.
I want you to enjoy a life of regret.

I want to give you all that you've given me,
Pain.

[Our Contract].

Either I hurt you,
or you hurt me.
Those are the terms of the contract.
These are non-negotiable.

Because when you love so immensely,
no one comes out unscathed,
there is no room for protection,
there is no opportunity to hold back.

Because when you love like this,
you believe that the pleasure,
is worth all the pain,
even though you know the pain will last longer.

Because when you love like this,
there is so much pain,
and it never, really, goes away.
It becomes a part of you.

What can I tell you
after having experienced a love like this?

Love anyway,
because this type of pain is one that very few
get the pleasure of knowing.

[Hopeless].

They consider hopelessness to be a pathetic, down-trotted, damnation of an existence.

As I look at all that has laid down and burned up before me,
Hopeless is everything that I wish I could be.

As I write this, I am laying in a dark bedroom,
alone,
Hallowing beneath the false security of blankets.
This patheticness has come to define my existence.

Hopelessness, now, seems to be my only escape,
for, I am imprisoned,
held captive by the shreds of hope that I, still, hold so dear.

Each day I tell myself to give up,
attempt to will myself to move on,
create mental notes of rationale that would support the idea of living a life without you.

I sound off, each day, a list of all your mistakes,
a long, detailed list of each instance you let me down,
and broke me beyond anything I feared you were capable of.

Still, I wish I was hopeless.
The truth is, I can't seem to find a way to let go of the little hope that remains.
This hope, truly, is all I have left of you.

And once this little hope that I hold so close to my heart,
withers, decays, and, inevitably, dies away,
I'm afraid of who I will be,
I'm afraid if I will be,
at all.

Something about you
must be unlike anything I've ever experienced,
because, despite every possible exit from this 'purgatory',
I don't wanna go.

I want to stay
with you.

And I wish I didn't,
I wish I could convince myself that this was all wrong,
I wish I could believe that this really is the end,
but I just can't.

And it's nights like these,
as I lay in an empty bed,
in a dark room,
without you,
wondering where you may be,
that I just want to be hopeless.

[Losing Sleep, Again].

Losing sleep, again,
Over the things that won't matter,
When I'm, finally, able,
To look back from a different place.

[One Last Wish].

You must have forgotten.
Oh, but I remember every word.

You called your lies playing it smart,
I called them deadly.
This was a case of manslaughter,
for this man is, indeed, slaughtered.

Dead and gone, never to return,
that is, never to return to you,
and never to return as the same.

You refuse to call your negligence a homicide,
on the grounds that it was unintentional,
but I think you knew what you were doing
all along.

At my funeral, I have arranged for you to read this,
One last letter.
It tells a story of love,
of pain and heartache,
of betrayal.

It is my hope,
that with this letter,
lessons will be learned.
Do not let my death go in vein.
Something must be gained here,
this is my only retribution.

And with my one, last dying wish,
I ask that you dig my grave.

It only seems appropriate.
There's a certain psychotic irony of it all.
You dug this pit for me, metaphorically.
Now, it's only right that you lay me down to a restless eternity,
literally.
With this literature,
I want your crimes to become literal.

But, don't worry, your secrets are safe with me.
The last remnants of your mistakes will die with me,
only to be remembered through these words in black and white,
on one last crumbled piece of loose leaf.

I'm taking them to my grave.
Your cover isn't blown,
nobody will know,
what you've done.

[Idols].

Little Johnny was only 6 years old,
out in the blistering cold,
waiting up for you,
but you never showed.

Shit, I used to love a song,
that resonated with me,
that went a little something like that.

But that was a lifetime ago,
that was a different life ago,
but not much has changed.

I'm still deciding whether that's a blessing or a curse.

You were like my fucking idol,
but, eventually,
I got tired of being lied to,
Neglected,
Pathetic.

Yeah, that's right,
now I get it.
I got tired of being pathetic.

A child's love for their "parents" is made to be unconditional,
but, in these conditions,
the outcome was pitiful.

So, I decided to stop all that I was doing.
You taught me, "only sissies cry",
so, I stopped crying.
You taught me how to lie,
so, I started lying.
You taught me how to be selfish,
so, I became that, too.

And, eventually,
I stopped caring about you.

[The Griever].

You don't love me.
It's okay,
I don't love you, either.
I've spent this life a Griever.

I'll always be a Griever,
telling myself I don't need her.
Cynical and mad,
over everything I never had.

'It's not her fault',
'She doesn't know any better'.
But I knew better.
You should have been better.

I should be better,
maybe it's the weather.
I've always hated November,
but that's no excuse to feel like this.

I'm stronger than this,
stronger than you,
stronger than everyone.
But, still, not strong enough for this.

That day, standing in front of a hole in the ground,
He told me to be strong for everyone else around.
I had to be strong for the weak,
but, who would be strong for me?
Nobody.

Since that day, that's what I've always done,
I've been strong for everyone.

Let me carry this Cross through the streets,
For all of you to see.
Ravage me with stones.
Cast me out and Crucify me in front of everyone.
This is what I need.

I needed a Purpose.
So my Purpose became to be a vessel of pain.
Let me harbor it.
Let me wallow in it.
It hurts just the way I want it to,
just the same as it always has.

You didn't love me,
And it's still okay.
Sadly, I wouldn't be here without you.
This has become my Purpose, now.
I'm a Griever.

Watch [Over Me].

It's *just* a watch,
but it's all I have left.

He was *just* a man,
but, he was all I had left.

I wear it every day.
I think of you every day.

I know you're not here anymore
to watch over me.
But, I'm hoping this artifact of you
is enough for me.

It's all I have left now.

I look at these golden links,
this white face,
the Roman Numerals around it's circumference.
Something about it is reassuring.
Something about it is comforting.
I need to find solace in this,
It's all I have left now.

Some days I feel silly,
looking for comfort in empty material.
My "logical" thinking,
tells me that I'm helplessly holding onto something,
that I know will never take your place,
that I know will never bring you back.

But, still, this watch is everything to me,
It's all I have left now.

Maybe I am silly,
maybe I am a fool.
But, can you blame me,
for so desperately trying to hold onto something?

We all need something,
we all need someone,
to hold onto.

I tried to hold onto you
for so long.
I'm, still, trying to hold on.

It's all I have left now.

[The Gift].

This is a story,
of two runaway trains.

One traveling at 100mph going east,
the other traveling at 100mph going west.

Both on track for a head-on collision,
but the outcome is not what you had expected.

When the prognosis was destruction,
the outcome was salvation.

I was the phony, dressed in a Knight's shining armor,
You were the outcast, labeled the kingdom's Jester.

They said we were never the same,
you thought we were never the same,
but I knew,
exactly what I was hiding,
&& exactly what you couldn't hide
from me.

You thought I was so strong,
Hell, everyone did.
But I kept it a secret,
that I always thought you were stronger.

I know how it sounds,
after everything, you probably still can't agree.
But I never had the balls to put that knife to my skin,
no matter how many times I thought about it.

But you did,
so that's gotta count for something.

They still don't see it,
and, maybe, you don't either.
Can't say I blame you,
I've been faking it for so long.

Some days I forget who I really am,
caught up in the inconsistencies of
what I showed,
and how I truly felt.

But I digress,
let us continue this pathological fairy tale.

I saw something in you,
that I buried deep within myself.
Something that I could only reveal
late at night,
in a dark, empty room,
with no one around to see.

I knew you were the same,
but I kept it a secret.

Our pain was the secret,
something so tormenting,
that brought us both
to each other's rescue.

I didn't want to scare you away.
Instead, I wanted to study you,
to examine exactly what it was that made us so similar,
yet. so different when it came to our roles in this misguided society.

You thought I was some kind of savior,
but, the truth is,
I didn't do any saving.

The truth is, I needed you more than you needed me.

All I needed to do was to show you,
that there was more out there than you thought,
to show you,
that despite what everyone saw,
despite what you thought,
despite what went on out there,
you still had everything I wanted.

The friendships meant nothing.
The girls meant nothing.
All of those superficial luxuries of a high school existence meant nothing to me,
but everything to you.

They say "the grass is always greener",
well, I'll be damned if they weren't right about that.

You had the family I always wanted,
a loving and full place to come home to everyday after school,
people who cared about you and showed you
what love really is.

I wanted some of that.
I needed some of that.

Just a little,
not too much.
I was hoping I could steal a few moments of that,
just to know what it was like,
to live like you.

You wanted to know what it was like to live like me.
But, to this day, I've still never showed you.

You might think that's selfish of me,
but, the truth is,
I was sparing you from the truth,
shielding you from
a truth that nobody wanted to see,
a truth that I just couldn't admit.

Sometimes we have to settle for those lies,
when the truth just isn't good enough.

But I've been working,
I've been trying
to give you a window
into this mess.

I didn't say it would be pretty,
in fact, it's pretty hideous
to have all of this,
all of these things that you thought you wanted.

There's a certain twisted irony to it all,
people believing something for so long,
gathering all of this falsified evidence,
provided by yours truly,
to mislead,
and to protect us both.

You were my best friend.
You, still, are my best friend,
and that's something that was always real.
I could never hide that.
I would never hide that.

And that's the moral of this story,
that things aren't always what they seem,
people aren't always as they seem.
This story contradicts all those fairy tales,
all those lies,
they told us as children.

Because, in this story,
the court's Jester saves the Knight,
from a life sentence,
of isolation and agony.

Despite what they saw,
despite what you saw,
you were my knight,
disguised as a Jester,
and I was the peasant,
pretending to play the part,
they said was right for me.

My only desire is that these words,
written on this page,
can, somehow, encapsulate what you mean to me,
can, somehow, reveal all that you've given me.

You gave me hope in the desolation of hopelessness.
You gave me direction when my compass was broken.
You, finally, gave me that love and family,
that I thought was a luxury for all but me.

Without all of these gifts,
I can assure you that I would not be here today.
I would have given up long ago,
probably falling victim to the same late night temptations that we both know so well.

So, I hope that you can rejoice with me,
share in the joy of my successes,
share in my process of healing,
because none of it would be without you.

And no matter where I go,
no matter how far I am,
your gifts live on through me.

What Will Become of Us? [Part I].

Born together,
Raised together,
Grown together,
Cried together.

Built together,
Learned together,
Failed together,
Overcame together.

Now, what will become of us?

Now on different paths,
part of me, still, doesn't understand it.

Yesterday, we were all the same,
riding our bikes together,
running from the police together,
staying out too late together,
getting too high together,
selling drugs together,
chasing girls together.

When did it all get so different?
How did it all get so different?

I, still, feel the same.
I, still, look at you all the same.
I don't see the differences,
but, I feel them.

Even after all the tragedies over the years,
I still feel the same.
None of that changed it for me.

Years,
Distance,
Money,
Divorce,
Addiction,
Theft,
Lies,
Rehab,
Overdose.

None of that changed any of you
in my eyes.

I've always been one to cling onto the past,
in an effort to escape the uncertainty
that the future holds.

So, maybe I am biased,
maybe I am afraid,
of the uncertainty,
of what will become of us.

I'm not good at letting go,
never have been.
Maybe because I've never had much to hold onto.
So, for the few that I hold so dear,
I have a tendency to hold on,
tight.

But, I can't hold on anymore.

Time is something we can't escape.
Progress is something we can't escape.
And, it is my time,
to go on and progress.

I should be happy.
They keep telling me,
that I should be happy.
Then, why aren't I happy?

Maybe I'm just caught up in my thoughts.

What will become of us?

Will I ever return?
Will there be anything to return to?

Maybe,
years from now,
for a funeral,
or an incarceration hearing,
or a bail out,
or, simply, to the remnants of friendships
that has been reduced to ash.

I hope not.
But, these are my thoughts,
these are my nightmares.

What will become of us?

What Will Become of Us? [Part II].

We don't choose our life,
&& we, most certainly, don't choose our family.

Sometimes I think life must be determined
by some kind of twisted roll of the dice,
or, maybe, a game of Russian Roulette.

Whatever or Whoever is responsible for this mess,
I have to thank Him.

Don't get me wrong,
I'd be lying if I said that I didn't want to give it another try,
another roll of the dice,
another spin of these loaded chambers,
just to see what it's like to live on the other side.

Another Life,
another Home,
another Family,
another Mother.

But I do owe him some gratitude,
for giving me just enough,
just enough of something,
that I didn't even know I needed.

Friends.
Friends turned into family.

They became my family
when the term 'Family' had been just a word to me,
just a foreign concept,
created by a stranger,
who knew nothing about my life,
who knew nothing about my existence.

Family,
they talked about it in school,
like it was some type of necessity,
some type of measure of the quality of a 'good' human.

Well, by that measure,
I fell pathetically short of expectations,
and that feeling never subsided,
that void remained noticeable,
remained apparent.

That feeling became fluid throughout my life.

But, as I said, I was given a blessing
that I didn't know was a blessing,
until it was already a part of my life.

We don't always choose our friends,
sometimes it's luck,
sometimes it's bad luck,
sometimes it's timing,
sometimes it's proximity.

Whatever the reason,
my friends were the blessing
that had remained disguised to me.

How was I so fortunate to grow up around these people
that, so effortlessly, shaped my existence,
sculpted my mind,
&& built my character.

I want to call it a true miracle of chance,
but the lesser half of me is compelled to validate,
'Well, I was owed this.
At least He gave me something.'

Although I'm biased,
maybe, that is true.

Yes, I was a poor man on many scales,
but I was rich in so many others.

No money,
but some friends to share this life with,
some people to lean on,
even if I never told them I needed them,
even if I never told them I was leaning,
even if I never showed them the things that remain hidden.

That is a luxury that I don't believe too many people have.
Well, maybe, "that's what family is for".
Well, I wouldn't know about that,
but, I do know what it's like to have some people
to call friends.

Friends that are there for you when you need them,
that let you sleep over when your mom is drunk, again,
that will hang out with you when you're all alone and nobody is home,
that call you to hang out on holidays,
knowing you're spending it alone,
and not with that beloved family everyone else has.

The same friends that let you play in the Father-and-Son Father's Day baseball game,
even though they know you don't have a Father.

I hope you can feel the love.
I hope my appreciation seeps through this page like some spilled coffee.

I hope I can make all of these emotions real to you,
despite being a man too afraid to show any emotion on the surface,
despite being a man who speaks about emotion, thought && feeling all day,
but, still can't find the courage to allow himself to participate without a barrier for protection.

I didn't choose my friends,
but I have some great ones,
The ones who grew up on the same block,
in the same town,
in the same life as me.

We are bonded forever,
whether you like it or not.
This is my reassurance
as I sit up late at night,
and wonder what will become of us...

[A Letter Never Sent].

Do you ever wonder about me,
entertaining the possibilities of who and what I have become after all these years?

You said you would come back to visit.
Foolishly, I believed you.

I waited outside every time for you,
but you never came back for me.

Don't you ever wonder about that little boy you left behind,
disposing of me from your life,
like Brenda's baby in the trash.

I already know the answer,
your absence says it all.

I just figured I'd ask,
in the event that my instincts are wrong,
in the event that you would tell me that you care,
in the slim chance that I matter, even the slightest, to you.

But, it's okay, I know better.
You don't care,
You never did,
and, now, neither do I.

In fact, I'll probably just throw this letter away,
just like all the others.

This will be just another,
Letter Never Sent.

[Free Byrd].

I'm a Free Byrd
of the free verse,

But these aren't free words,
they came at the price
of a mean hurt.

I want to fly away,
I don't need earth.

She's a Black Death,
like a clean hearse.

I look at her,
& don't see worth,

so, I walk away,
& I leave her.

I tried to stay,
but it won't work.

They called it Love,
but it's a cruel curse.

You'll never know real hurt,
like the heartbreak
from your first.

[Just Words].

I give these words life.
But, they're just words to you,
You don't know what they mean to me.

[X].

"I think **I'll let you go** [inside] **now.**"

Appendix:

1. [The Prelude].
2. [No].
3. [Desecration].
4. [Broken Together].
5. [Growing Pains].
6. [Wisdom].
7. [Courage].
8. [Plans Go Awry].
9. [Villain].
10. [Just a Little].
11. [The Anarchist].
12. [Innocent Lost].
13. [Slipping away...].
14. [Voluntary Slavery].
15. [Unstable].
16. [The Price of Poetry].
17. [Broken Pieces].
18. [Masks].
19. [Fearful Inhibitions].
20. [Inspiration].
21. [Blank].
22. [22].
23. [Darker].
24. [Fit in].
25. [Martyr].
26. [Self-Destructive].
27. [Re-finding What was Lost].
28. [One Man Can Change].
29. They [Left].
30. [Self-Deprecation].

31. [Scars].
32. [Brainwashed].
33. [Free-Will].
34. [Impermanence].
35. [Strength].
36. [The Rush of Uncertainty].
37. [Running].
38. [Peaks && Valleys].
39. [High tide].
40. [Lost && Found].
41. [Low tide].
42. [Proverbs I].
43. [The Battle].
44. [Victim].
45. [Do you still remember?].
46. [Thief].
47. [Never Came Back].
48. [Love&War].
49. [Now&Then].
50. [50].
51. [The 5th].
52. [Then, Gone].
53. [Cold].
54. [Proverbs II].
55. [Proverbs III].
56. [Denial].
57. [Loose Ends].
58. [Always, Always].
59. [Onions].
60. [Reflection].
61. [Time].

62. [No More].
63. [Pain].
64. [Our contract].
65. [Hopeless].
66. [Losing Sleep, Again].
67. [One Last Wish].
68. [Idols].
69. [The Griever].
70. Watch [Over Me].
71. [The Gift].
72. What Will Become of Us? [Part I].
73. What Will Become of Us? [Part II].
74. [A Letter Never Sent].
75. [Free Byrd].
76. [Just Words].
77. [X].

www.ingramcontent.com/pod-product-compliance
Lightning Source LLC
Chambersburg PA
CBHW040847170426
43201CB00005BB/45